AR 2.4

17.95

ANIMAL
SUPERPOWERS

ALLIGATOR

JOSH PLATTNER

CONSULTING EDITOR, DIANE CRAIG, M.A./READING SPECIALIST

Super Sandcastle

An Imprint of Abdo Publishing
abdopublishing.com

abdopublishing.com

Published by Abdo Publishing, a division of ABDO, PO Box 398166, Minneapolis, Minnesota 55439. Copyright © 2016 by Abdo Consulting Group, Inc. International copyrights reserved in all countries. No part of this book may be reproduced in any form without written permission from the publisher. Super SandCastle™ is a trademark and logo of Abdo Publishing.

Printed in the United States of America, North Mankato, Minnesota
062015
092015

THIS BOOK CONTAINS RECYCLED MATERIALS

Editor: Liz Salzmann
Content Developer: Nancy Tuminelly
Cover and Interior Design and Production: Anders Hanson, Mighty Media, Inc.
Photo Credits: Shutterstock

Library of Congress Cataloging-in-Publication Data
Plattner, Josh, author.
 Alligator : master of might / Josh Plattner ; consulting editor, Diane Craig, M.A./reading specialist.
     pages cm. -- (Animal superpowers)
 Audience: K to grade 4
 ISBN 978-1-62403-735-1
 1. Alligators--Juvenile literature. I. Title.
 QL666.C925P62 2016
 597.98'4--dc23
                       2014048270

Super SandCastle™ books are created by a team of professional educators, reading specialists, and content developers around five essential components— phonemic awareness, phonics, vocabulary, text comprehension, and fluency—to assist young readers as they develop reading skills and strategies and increase their general knowledge. All books are written, reviewed, and leveled for guided reading, early reading intervention, and Accelerated Reader™ programs for use in shared, guided, and independent reading and writing activities to support a balanced approach to literacy instruction.

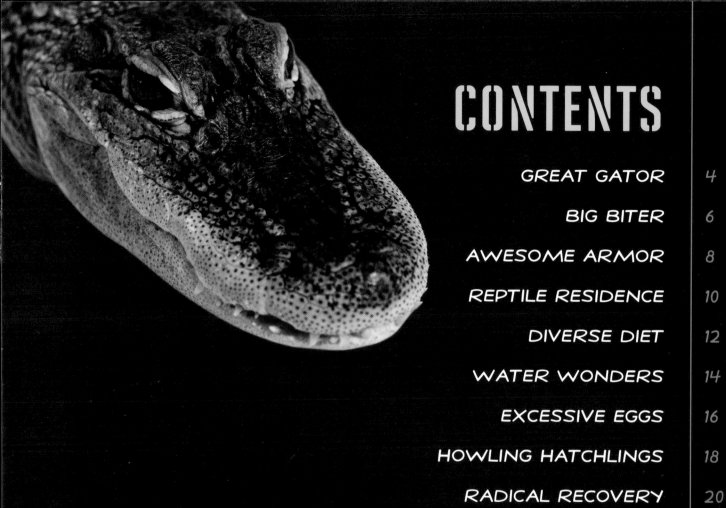

CONTENTS

GREAT GATOR

American alligators are large reptiles. They are longer than 13 feet (4.0 m). They weigh more than 750 pounds (340 kg).

Their tails are strong and flat.

BIG BITER

What is this animal's superpower? Biting! Alligators have powerful jaws.

THE STRONGEST BITE

They have the strongest bite in the world. It is four times stronger than a great white shark's.

AWESOME ARMOR

Alligators look like they have armor. They have bony plates under their skin.

These plates are called scutes.

REPTILE RESIDENCE

Alligators live near freshwater. Most alligators live in swamps.

Alligators also live near **marshes** and slow-moving rivers.

DIVERSE DIET

Alligators will eat almost anything. They feed on turtles, fish, and small **mammals**. If they are really hungry, they'll eat dead animals.

AN ALLIGATOR EATING A CRAB

Watch out. Sometimes they eat humans!

WATER WONDERS

On land, alligators are **clumsy**. They are heavy and slow.

In water, they are **dangerous**. They swim very quickly.

EXCESSIVE EGGS

Female alligators lay 35 to 50 eggs. Some lay more than 80!

COVERING THE EGGS

Adult alligators cover their nests with grass and leaves.

The eggs stay covered for two months.

HOWLING HATCHLINGS

Baby alligators make loud **squeals** inside their eggs. This happens right before they hatch.

HATCHLING SIZE

They are 6 to 8 inches (15 to 20 cm) long.

Young alligators grow 12 inches (30 cm) each year.

RADICAL RECOVERY

Alligators are hunted for their skin. Some are hunted for their meat. They were **endangered** in the United States. They were added to the list of protected animals.

Thanks to this protection, they are no longer **endangered**.

ALLIGATOR SUPERHERO

Can you imagine
an alligator
superhero?
What would
it look like?
What could
it do?

WHAT DO YOU KNOW ABOUT
ALLIGATORS?

1. An alligator's superpower is swimming.

TRUE OR FALSE?

2. Alligators will eat almost anything.

TRUE OR FALSE?

3. Female alligators lay 35 to 50 eggs.

TRUE OR FALSE?

4. Alligators are still **endangered**.

TRUE OR FALSE?

ANSWERS:
1. FALSE 2. TRUE 3. TRUE 4. FALSE

GLOSSARY

CLUMSY - awkward and lacking grace.

DANGEROUS - able or likely to cause harm or injury.

ENDANGERED - having few left in the world.

MAMMAL - a warm-blooded animal that has hair and whose females produce milk to feed their young.

MARSH - a low area of soft, wet land.

SQUEAL - a high-pitched cry or sound.